Acknowledgment

Thanks to those who submitted their anonymous entries.
May your voices be heard.

Special Thanks to my family for their endless support
and
as always to G_d

Table of Contents

Chapter 1: Misunderstood in Middle School

My name is Pebble. I wake up every day and go to school. I like to read, play the piano and chew lots of bubble gum. I live at home with my parents and my older brother Joseph. We are a small but close family. My mother has been sick for a very long time. When I was young, she was in a car accident and has been in a wheel chair ever since. She needs help to eat, to brush her teeth, and to get dressed because she is a quadriplegic; the doctor says that she is paralyzed from her neck to her toes. My father works two jobs; during the day he is a lawyer and at night he is a sports referee. He is always at work, I miss him very much.

At school, I do not have many friends because the students can be very mean and I am very shy. Often, I share the cookies I buy at school for snack with my friend Adrianne. She walks with me every day to lunch. Adrianne is very kind and she helps me with the notes in class. Going to school would be much easier if my teacher would review the work, and did not move on to the next chapter until the materials were learned. My class is often loud which makes it hard to concentrate.

I wonder if my teacher, Ms. Scott cares about me. Especially, when I try talking with her after a lesson and she ignores me while she shuffles through her bag to get ready for lunch. I asked Ms. Scott if I can come back after school to get help with math since I do not understand the material. I am performing poorly on my tests and quizzes. Ms. Scott says, she does not get paid after dismissal and quickly walks away. When she does this, I feel like she does not care about how I perform in school. Sometimes it makes me wonder why I should try so hard to get good grades in class.

When my father comes in to say goodnight, we talk about how my teacher makes me feel. He said it is important that I ask questions and work really hard at school. I explain to my father how the work assignments in math and science classes are confusing; I get really shy and too embarrassed to ask my teacher for assistance.

When the class gets to loud, Ms. Scott sits in her favorite rocking chair which she pulls out from underneath the corner of the smart board. She does this instead of answering questions and trying to calm the class down. When I tell my father it makes him very angry. He has called the principal before and was told that it would be taken care of. He has no time to come to my school because he is always working. I told my father that I do not want him to tell my teacher how I feel because I do not want Ms. Scott to be mad at me.

I often feel like going over to my teacher's desk to ask her questions during quiet work time, but often she is on her cell phone and I do not want to disturb her. My teachers always seem to be in a good mood on Fridays. On Fridays, the teachers always seem to have a smile on their faces, they play more fun activities in class and they give us extra free time. I like to go to school on Fridays because all the teachers are friendlier to me.

The best part about Fridays is that my friend Adrianne and I have Physical Education. I like this class a lot because we get to exercise and have fun. My Physical Education teacher does not need a smart board or a black board to write on, or hand out tests. He demonstrates the activities and then we perform the activities in our groups.
I like Saturdays because I spend time with my grandparents. Grandpa tries to help me with my questions and homework from school. It is difficult for him sometimes because my school work is very different from what Grandpa learned in school.

On Monday, I brought my homework to Ms. Scott, her coffee spilled all over it. I am sure all the answers were correct. I worked really hard on my homework with grandpa. My teacher apologized and told me not to worry. It makes me upset since the class rule is *no drinking or eating*, but it was okay for Ms. Scott to drink in class.

It was nice to see my teacher smile Tuesday morning. However, there is a misbehaved student in my class, his name is Jacques. He misbehaves a lot. He usually throws pencils and other things across the room. I hope he will not throw anything across the room today because I have to see my mother at the hospital after school and I want to be in a good mood. I feel really sad when the teacher punishes the whole class for Jacques' misbehaviors; that is not fair. I wonder how my teacher would feel if one teacher showed up late to school and our principal asked all of the teachers to stay after school as a punishment. Since, she often punishes the whole class for one student's bad behavior.

I can barely wait for Wednesday. I will meet with Ms. Believe; my English teacher, Mr. Lavie; my French teacher, Miss Core; my School Psychologist, and Mrs. Belle; my School Counselor. We have a lunch meeting to talk about what is important to me. They really care about my feelings and my academic success. They give me a desk and quiet time that allows me to do my homework when I cannot focus in the class; especially when other students are being disruptive.

I am worried! My teachers are very anxious because on Thursday we have to take a test. The class was told that our grade will be a reflection of how well we were taught and learned the material. I have been so nervous; I went to the nurse's office because I feel like I have butterflies in my stomach. Since I have not retained all the equations, I am more nervous than my teachers. I get confused and forget my math facts by the time I memorize the equations. In science, the formulas are extensive; they are very difficult to remember.

Since everyone is so stressed, there are a lot of fights in our school. One of the boys who were involved, Jared, pulled my lunch line buddy to the ground by her hair. I ran over and helped her up. I reported the incident to the monitor who was supposed to watch us during recess. The lunch monitor did not see the incident because she was talking with another teacher. When they asked Jared about the incident, he lied. How can they believe him? He always gets in trouble.

I asked to go to the nurse's office, but instead I went to the principal's office. Mr. Samuel asked me to explain why I was in his office with a nurse's pass? I told him Jared pulled my friend to the ground by her hair and the teacher did not believe me. I told him that Jared lied and has been bullying myself and other students. Mr. Samuel said that he knows Jared's family and that he will take care of it. Later, on my way to music class, Jared pointed his tongue at me and screamed out loud, "My father plays golf with Mr. Samuel every Saturday, tattle tale!"

I told Jared that he pulled my friend down by her hair and that it was not nice to do that. Jared yelled at me and said he was going to fight me. I told him that he was a bully and that if he did not stop I would tell Ms. Scott. Jared just laughed at me. Immediately after saying this, I saw Ms. Scott walking out of our classroom; she looked at me, Jared and the ten students that were around us, she turned around and walked in the other direction while talking on her cell phone. Jared noticed Ms. Scott and laughed again in my face then pushed me to the floor. I picked myself off the floor and walked away.
I decided that there was no hope, no forgiveness, no fairness, no justice, no way out for me at school.

One day, I will become a superstar teacher. I will help every student and listen when they ask me questions. I only wish Jared's parents would teach him how to be respectful to other people. I wonder if Jared gets enough attention at home since he consistently talks in class about his new video game, and how his father is always golfing and his mother is always shopping and hanging out with her friends. I hope that Jacques parents' teach him to behave well in class.

Pebble's Promise

One day, I will be a great teacher in class just like the astronauts who walk on the moon.
One day, I will take and keep my oath as a teacher just like a surgeon does before operating on a patient
One day, I will teach a classroom and work hard even when no one is watching or asking for assistance.
One day, I will get to know my students as if they were my own children
One day, I will help my students when they need it without questioning their ability
One day, I will take timeless pride in all the minds I teach rather than watching the clock tick by
One day, I will hold a child's hand and teach them how to write and read without judgment
One day, I will not ask why, but how can I help?
One day, I will put students before myself
One day, I will lead and have many followers

Unfortunately, Pebble was not able to fulfill her dreams for becoming a star teacher. She committed suicide almost a year after this poem was written.

Chapter 2: I Made it Against the Odds

Middle school was a difficult time for me. The other kids did not like me because I was not popular. I studied diligently, so I did not have time to hang out with other kids my age.

I remember, one day in the fall when I was working on my math homework at lunch time. I rarely sat to eat. A girl named Sarah, whom, I thought was my friend came to my table; sat down and smiled at me. I will never forget when Sarah took a moment of silence, then cocked her head to the side and said "You might as well kill yourself, you'll never have friends." I was stunned; I stared at her with a calm face, trying so hard not to react to her words. I had found out years before that if a bully notices that the victim is not upset, they may go away. I took a deep breath and went back to my work with a heavy heart.

A few days after the incident, I was called down to the counseling center. I sat at the low, tan table, eating my bright red apple without a care in the world. As far as I knew, I had done nothing wrong and nothing was wrong with me, so there was no reason to be nervous. The counselor looked at me with a genuine smile. She asked how I was doing, if I had been depressed lately. She knew me since I visited her many times before. The counseling center was where I usually ate lunch when the teasing and taunting became too much for me. I told her I was the same as usual with a slight shrug of my shoulder. The counselor gave me a sad smile and nodded in understanding.

She looked serious all of the sudden, which made me sit up straight in the dark blue chair. "I was told that you were talking about killing yourself" she said calmly. I looked down at the table and cried openly in front of her; I emptied my soul in tears. I knew where the rumor was coming from; it was said to me by Sarah. I began to blubber out broken sentences, trying to explain to her what happened, and where the harsh words had come from.

The counselor handed me a facial tissue so that I could dry my tears, hugged me tight, and softly rubbed my back. I felt that she understood the pain that I was feeling. Once the tears had slowed, she explained to me that she would have to call my parents and tell them what happened. I cried even more, afraid that my parents would believe the rumors.

As she sat beside me; my weak and battered mind understood that she was allowing me the opportunity to tell my parents my side of the story. Although I tried to tell my parents my side of the story on the phone, I did not accomplish this goal. Since I was not speaking in coherent sentences my counselor took the phone and discussed what she knew about my current situation with my parents.

After I calmed down, I was able to return to class and agreed to meet with my instigator the following day in her office.

The rest of that school day was a blur. I recall walking home, knowing that I would not cry. I convinced myself that it was just another day and everything would be alright. My father met me at the door to our white, two-story home and held me to his chest. I recall his soothing words but I could not stay focused. I sat with my parents and dictated to them the events of the day and the impending meeting with the bully.

I recall that the first meeting with Sarah took place the next morning. She sat across from me beside her friends with a smug grin of self-satisfaction. I remember she denied everything; as her friends denied ever hearing the rumor. Later on, my counselor discovered Sarah's friends partook in the rumor as well. She suggested we all stay away from one another. We did not share the same classes so the chances of us seeing one another became very slim. The avoidance policy stuck with us through high school.

In the end, you can become friends with some bullies; however, it does not always turn out that way. It is important to understand that you cannot change the bully. All you can do is be strong and seek help.

Chapter 3:   I am Not Popular but I am Unique

Ten year old Harold was very smart and polite. He had a contagious smile that made everyone's day. He had bright green eyes and a mop of dark brown hair that brushed over his shoulders; he thought he was very handsome. Harold learned from his after-school teacher, Mrs. Zeller, to always follow the golden rule; do onto others as you would want others to do onto you.

Although Harold was quite happy in most of his classes, he often felt upset and depressed on his way to his least favorite class, Physical Education. The other students in Physical Education gave Harold the nickname "Huge Harry". Harold was not very tall; he was called huge because he was overweight.

During Physical Education, the other students would pick their friends to play on their team. They left Harold to be the last one picked for every game. This made him very sad. He was good at most sports and enjoyed running and playing games. When he was the last student standing against the bleachers of the tan gym waiting to be picked, he would simply shuffle his feet and look up sadly at his teacher. Mr. Palmer shook his head knowing how Harold must have felt.

Harold had been feeling worse since a new student named Corey started last week. Corey was an active 11 year old in the 5th grade who moved in from another state. He was good at all the games that the students played. When they played baseball, he got a home run every time. In basketball, he shot all three pointers without an issue. When they had races, he was always first across the finish line and cheered for Harold's classmates as they crossed after him. As nice as he was to all the other students, he constantly teased Harold about his weight. Some of the other students had begun picking on Harold since Corey arrived.

Corey had become friends with some of Harold's classmates who started to call him fat, ugly and dumb. Harold knew that this had to stop. He was never that bad at sports, he never got as many home runs or came in first place like Corey did; he always tried his best. He told his teacher, Mrs. Zeller, during their afternoon study session about how the students were hurting his feelings and how frustrated he was with always being picked last in gym. Mrs. Zeller told Harold that some people do not respect others or follow the golden rule. She told him that sometimes they are trying to fit in with the other students. They sometimes follow bad examples in order to seem cool and avoid being bullied by the other students. Harold's eyes began to tear up.

He asked Mrs. Zeller why they always picked on him. He was never disrespectful to the other students. He did not understand why they had to be so hurtful; he just wanted it to stop. She gave him a hug and with a pat on the back and told him he was a wonderful person. She promised to talk with a good friend of hers that may be able to help. Harold sadly returned the hug and thanked Mrs. Zeller. Later, that afternoon Mrs. Zeller met with Mr. Palmer, she told him about Harold's situation. Mr. Palmer said he noticed that Harold had been sad and had an idea to help Harold feel better.

The next day, while in Physical Education class, Mr. Palmer decided to choose the teams himself. There would be no more team captains. He stood at the head of the gym and said anyone wearing a blue shirt, white shorts or black socks would be on team one. Those in grey shirts, black shoes or white socks would be on team two.
Before Harold knew it the teams were picked and he was not picked last. Mr. Palmer had a plan; he knew that Harold's favorite two sports were football and basketball. Mr. Palmer chose basketball for the sport of the day. He then chose Harold's team to play Corey's team in the first game. In the past, Harold did not get many opportunities to play in the game because the captains always chose the players, but today, he played as much as anyone else.

To everyone's surprise Harold was a great basketball player. He could dribble, pass, and shoot as well as Corey. During the game he passed the ball to his teammates and made several shots. His teammates were very happy that he was on their team. Even the other team gave Harold high fives after the game ended. This experience made him feel very good inside.

Harold felt proud of his abilities and for the first time all year he felt accepted by his peers. Unfortunately, Corey still picked on Harold saying he got lucky and he was still fat, ugly and dumb in the locker room. The other boys looked away, afraid of Corey calling them names as well. Harold knew he was overweight and thought he was good looking and he definitely knew he was smart. He decided to work on the one thing that he knew he could change; his weight.

Harold decided to talk with Mr. Palmer about his weight. It was easy to talk to Mr. Palmer because he respected him for being a great teacher and a wonderful person. Mr. Palmer sat with him during lunch and discussed the different ways he could control his weight. They talked about eating healthier foods and becoming more active on a daily basis. Then Mr. Palmer remembered Harold's second favorite sport; football. Mr. Palmer knew that the school year was coming to an end and they would have to come up with a plan that would help Harold achieve his goal of losing weight over the summer.

Mr. Palmer was the coach for the summer football team. He asked him to run and to exercise with him after school. He asked him to eat healthier and to continue being a great student. He then told Harold that if he can eat healthy, run and be active everyday he would be able to play on his football team.

Starting the very next day, Harold walked to school instead of taking the bus. After a week, he was able to walk even faster and soon he was able to jog to school. On the last week before summer vacation, he ran!

Mr. Palmer noticed Harold jogging to school and was amazed. He asked Harold to stop in his office during lunch so they could talk about his progress. He agreed and was excited to meet with Mr. Palmer. It had been almost two months since he decided to lose weight. When it was lunch time, Harold brought his lunch to meet with Mr. Palmer. He invited him into the office and they began to eat lunch together. Harold had a turkey sandwich on wheat bread, a yogurt, an apple, celery and carrots with a bottle of water.

Mr. Palmer was impressed with Harold's commitment to losing weight, not only had he began jogging to school but he was eating a healthy lunch. Mr. Palmer exclaimed, "You look great Harold, I am so proud of you". How are you doing? Do you still want to play football this summer? Harold stood up with excitement, and said in a raised voice "I would love to play! When does practice begin?" Mr. Palmer smiled and told Harold "I think you already have." He asked Mr. Palmer how he knew, but before he could respond Harold replied "oh, I know, I started to eat healthier and I started to exercise every day." "Exactly", said Mr. Palmer with a hearty handshake and a hi-five. He handed a practice schedule and forms for his parents to sign so he could play football. The lunch bell rang and he thanked Mr. Palmer and they agreed to see each other again on the football field.

Harold continued to eat healthy and exercise every day and when the first day of football practice came, he was ready. To his surprise there were a lot of boys from his school at the practice and there were plenty of boys he did not know. Corey was there and as soon as he saw Harold he began to call him "Huge Harry". *Oh no!* Harold thought, this bullying and teasing will never end. Harold ignored Corey and lined up for attendance and stretching. When Mr. Palmer started practice he placed the players in groups. Harold and Corey were in separate groups. The players started running drills and he was just as fast as Corey. Then the players were throwing the football and Harold could throw the ball as far as the other players and when they were catching the ball, Harold was the best! All of the other players were cheering for Harold except for Corey.

"You are still fat, ugly, and dumb," jeered Corey. Harold did not let it hurt his feelings because he knew that he lost weight, and he knew that he was not ugly and he knew that he was very smart. As the next few weeks passed all of the other players were impressed with Harold and wanted to be his friend, except for Corey. He still taunted and made fun of Harold. Corey continued to call Harold "Huge Harry." He would try to ignore the insults but he was getting frustrated at the constant belittling. The time had come for the players to wear football pads and begin tackling. Corey thought this is it; this is the time I will be able to show everyone how much better I am than "Huge Harry."

The team was performing a tackling drill; they used proper technique to tackle an opposing player. "Finally", Corey exclaimed loudly as he was lined up across from Harold. Mr. Palmer reminded both Corey and Harold that they were to use good technique in this drill. The boys lined up facing one another. Apprehension leaked through the sweat dripping down Harold's face. Corey gritted his teeth and got down low.

Mr. Palmer blew the whistle and the two boys ran toward each other, their shoulders hulked down and collided with an earth shattering slam. Harold opened his eyes and scrambled away quickly. He jogged back to the line to see a struggling Corey breathless on the ground. All the other players were clapping and cheering Harold! Harold! Harold!

He jogged back to where Corey was laying on the ground to offer his hand to Corey, helping him up. To his surprise Corey grabbed Harold's hand and stood up. Corey said "Nice tackle Harold." Harold said with an appreciative grin, "You can call me Huge Harry." From that day, Harold was known as "Huge Harry", not because he was fat, ugly, or dumb, but because he was someone to be proud of.

Chapter 4: I Had no Friends Except Myself

My name is Luniette. I grew up in different countries because my father was in the service. I liked playing the flute on rainy days and the piano on the weekends. I made many friends in my international schools abroad. I went to an all girls' school. The boys' international school was right across from mine and the boys were very respectful and kind to one another. The boys and girls only saw each other during religious ceremonies.

I went to school six days a week and for long periods of time. I loved Social Studies, Language, Science and Math. My friends and I had many things in common. We were academic friends and we enjoyed it very much. During lunch I would get picked up from school by my mother, my older brother or a chauffeur to drop me home. At home my mother would cook delicious meals. After eating, I would return to school to finish the day.

My favorite meal was Red Snapper, with lima bean soup, brown rice, and watercress on the side. After I ate all my food; mother would have apples from the United States of America. They were always so much bigger and tasted different from the apples grown on the island or the other countries I visited.

One day, my father announced that we will be moving again, this time to New York. I have traveled a lot internationally and lived in many different places around the world. I wondered if this was the last move. It was exciting to know that I will once again make new friends and meet new and nice people in New York. My father said I will start going to school and that the school system in New York will be different then what I am used to. In my mind, different was always a good thing.

When I arrived at school in New York, I realized that the students in class were very loud and I was not sure how I would fit in. I used to walk in the hallways and be extremely quiet in class, respect my teachers and make no sounds while the teachers were teaching. I noticed, everyone was in a rush but was not sure as to why. There was a loud bell that signified it was time to be in class; otherwise the students would be late. I used to look at my watch and memorize what time I had to be in class.

I also realized a lot of people only spoke one language; however I spoke three languages. I was told by my teacher I would be placed in a class called ESL for English as a Second Language. It was a very small class and I remembered one other student named Josette from Europe who spoke French and the other students' were fluent Spanish speakers. I did not like that class because the teacher spoke two languages; French and Spanish but with a different dialect. It made it difficult to translate the words in English.

There were students from other classes who occasionally passed by our class and pointed at us while the door was open; "They're learning English!" they would shout for the whole school to hear. It made me feel like it was a bad thing to learn. Learning is great and no matter what someone learns, it should be fun and enlightening.

At lunch time, I sat by myself since Josette had to get extra help with her homework. I had the table all to myself and no one ever bothered me. The Spanish speaking students were sitting together since they were friends from the previous year. It felt very lonely to sit by myself, so I studied while I was eating.

In the bathroom, a few fluent English speaking students asked me for my name. It was a happy time for me because they looked very friendly and they were smiling. Smiling is how we welcome friends, loved ones and people we care about in my country. I was wrong in that situation.

As I told them my name, one of the girls from the group pushed me and said, "Ha-ha, what kind of name is that?!" You are a pair of glasses, are you blind?" I told them my name was not glasses, that is was Luniette. Even in French, the word lunette for glasses was spelled differently. I ran out of the bathroom with tears running down my face and I decided they had no intention of becoming my friends. The days felt long and I had a heavy feeling in my heart that school would certainly be different but in a very sad way.

I did not have a chauffeur or my parents to pick me up from school anymore. I learned to take the bus, a taxi or walk to the next bus stop if I missed one. I would miss the bus almost every day because of the bullies at my new school. They would wait for me at the bus stop and sing my name out loud, "Luniette, Luniette, Luniette! Come over here, glasses!" So I would always walk to the second bus station. The buses were always crowded.

The travelers were always serious. Often, I would get up and offer my seat to an older person, a pregnant woman or a young child. It was enjoyable to travel by bus because I had the chance to think about school, there were no bullies and I got a chance to study.

The next day, my name was called over the loud speaker to go see the school Guidance Counselor. Some of the students started to chuckle but the teacher told them to stop it. Cowardly, I approached my teacher's desk and she handed me a pass to go to the guidance office.

I was scared and hoped that the girls who teased me would not be in the hallway. When I got to the guidance office; Mrs. Swartz, greeted me with a smile and welcomed me in. She asked me how I liked the school; I told her that I liked the teachers and the books but the students were mean.

Mrs. Swartz told me that I passed my language test and no longer needed to be in the ESL class. I shared with her that it was a requirement in my past school to learn English as well as other languages. She smiled and told me that I can continue getting help if I need to but I will have a full schedule complete with Math, Science, Social studies, and Physical Education. She explained that I could join positive students on the sports team and the Arts program as well.

I went back to class skipping happily and could not wait to get home to share the good news with my parents. My father said that I could continue playing the piano and try cheerleading if I chose to. My music teacher Mrs. Parrow was very patient with me. She respected me; she liked my name and knew a lot about other cultures. She made me very happy to be in New York and to be in a new school.

On Fridays, I had to stay after for cheerleading practice. While I was in the locker room; one of the girls from the cheerleading team approached me and told me that I had to wear a certain pair of glasses to be on the team. She handed me an extremely large pair of black plastic clown glasses with an attached moustache to wear. I was not sure what to do, so I took them and wore them.

Everyone was laughing at me while I was walking through the school. The school days felt long and endless. The pain that I felt was unbearable. Finally, I got to the track area were some other sports activities were in progress. Some students were running and others were clapping for their team. One of the athletes asked me if I was okay and that I can stay with them until the cheerleaders arrived. I felt elated. She asked me why I was wearing the clown-mustache glasses; I told her one of the cheerleaders told me it was a requirement to be on the team. She said, that was bullying and she would tell the coach.

I looked across the field and saw my squad gathering in the center. I hurried back to meet them. Since I was the smallest girl, the captain decided I would be the top of the pyramid. During practice, some of them were whispering to each other.

During this drill, I decided to remove these awful glasses. As the practice continued, the coach instructed the girls to catch me from the air. I felt a rush of fear, tears ran down my face and I asked Coach Jones to please give me a different position. He hugged me and said okay. The girls murmured "Oh, poor lunette, ha-ha". During practice, they pulled my hair band from my pony tail and I was not able to see the middle stance for my foot position and fell on my rear to the ground.

I was very upset with the actions of the cheerleading team and decided to speak with my music teacher. It was great to speak with Mrs. Parrow, she advised me to join the track and field team instead of staying on the cheer team. The track and field coach spoke with the cheerleading coach and I was able to join the track and field team the following week.

I was excited to start a new week of school since I was going to be in a class full of regular students; no more small group classes. I handed in all my homework every day. I used to always be first in my class internationally and was second twice which was devastating to me. I did not want to disappoint myself or my family. I held high expectations for myself.

I learned about Celsius in my country but that was not helpful here since the students in my study group had to teach me Fahrenheit and I would teach them how to study through decoding memorization; using the Latin language to memorize definitions. Since, I had been taught Latin; I knew there were many words that were easily decodable. My past school taught me to read and memorize two - three chapters of individual subjects for lectures or presentation.

I ate by myself four days out of the week. On Fridays, the music students and track team ate lunch with me in the cafeteria. Diane, Sue, and Patricia were my three best academic friends and also ate lunch with me Fridays.

The one Friday that my friends were not able to eat lunch with me, a few girls stopped by my lunch table and asked me to stop looking over at their table because their boyfriends were over there. Since I had no intention of becoming a problem and I held absolutely no interest in their boyfriends; I turned around, readjusted myself and faced the cafeteria wall.

Next thing I knew, two other girls approached me. One stood over the table and said "Hey, smarty pants, you will write our essay for us." I said "No, that is cheating." They quietly walked away as the lunch monitor approached the table.

As I looked out the window; it started snowing and I was secretly praying in my heart to get home safely. I was tired of being attacked by the other girls. As I rushed to my locker to get my coat, two of the girls escorted me outside and said "How about the essay?" They stood on either side of me and carried me from underneath my arms, dragging me outside on the snowy field as I screamed for help hoping someone would hear my cries.

The only thing I saw above was a cloudy snowy blue sky, I smelt the crisp cold air and felt the wetness from the melted snow on my clothes as they laughed hysterically while repeating "help me, help me," using mocking childish voices.

A third girl said "Let her go, she is part of the track team. Do not hurt her." They both dropped me and ran away as they left me lying in a pile of snow. My fear was telling my parents. I did not want them to worry about me. I said nothing to anyone about the incident. But, I relived this nightmare every day I walked into the school.

I decided if I colored my hair and changed my style the bullies would leave me alone. My parents always gave me money for allowance. One day, I decided I was going to buy my own clothes and change my style instead of wearing the European, handmade or Italian designer fashions that were bought for me. Since it felt like I had very few friends, I thought being smart had caused me to have more enemies.

I resolute to stop reading assigned chapters ahead of the class. My teacher at the time did not like that approach anyway. She once told me to wait for the class to complete their chapter's assignment before I could proceed to the next one. At the time, I figured why not read ahead and do my homework in advance.

The following weekend, I purchased a bottle of hair bleach and when my mother went to church; I took it upon myself and bleached my hair blonde. I also went to one of the local accessory stores and bought hoop earrings with glittery designs. My pants were skinny jeans with yellow and black tiger prints. I managed to save enough money and bought a pair of high top L.A. Gear and Reebok sneakers for daily wear instead of shoes.

Although I was allergic to certain makeup ingredients; I asked my friend Patricia if I could use some of her makeup. The popular bullies wore lots of makeup, had long blond hair and wore trendy animal print clothing. My parents were unhappy and disappointed with my new look. My three friends were worried that something was happening and I was not telling them.

All this effort to fit in made me feel even worse and sad inside. I became a loner and a shadow of myself. Track and field became the happiest activity for me. I learned that the best part about that sport was I could run as a team or alone. Not long after, I began running the track alone. It felt good, like freedom, the sounds of the wind, the palpitation of my heart beat, the thump of my feet grazing across the track, the scent of flowers, the pleasant presentation of the pines and the trees surrounding my circle of run. The sense of being in control of my destination was perfect.

It was me, the wind speed, the air that I breathed, and the circular endless track that brought me peace and happiness from the world that I saw through the eyes of a victim. While running toward the fence I decided to change further. Today, I changed my name to Luna. No longer do I participate in cheerleading, but I am captain of the debate team and I am in college to become a lawyer.

"Every night before I lay down to sleep; I pray and hope that the few teachers that share my world become bright stars in the sky and multiply into billions. These few teachers will light up the dark sky. I will not be afraid because I know all I have to do is look up, and there they will be." *Immaculine Jolivert* *age 12*

www.ingramcontent.com/pod-product-compliance
Lightning Source LLC
LaVergne TN
LVHW010029070426
835513LV00001B/32